WALKING

Walking, walking, what did I see?
A slithery snail stopped and said to me,
"What came first – me or my shell?"
I looked very hard but I couldn't tell.

1

Garden Snails

Garden snails lay their eggs in the ground. Inside the eggs the tiny snails start to form. When they hatch, their shells are almost transparent, but they look just like the adult snails. As they grow, their shells grow, too.

In winter, or when the weather is very cold or dry, the snail pulls its body inside its shell and seals the opening with a plug of slime. Snails live about three to five years.

2

3

Walking, walking, what did I see?
A black-back gull squawked at me,
"How did my wing feathers get to be black?
Once I had speckles all over my back."

Black-back Gull

The black-back gull lays its eggs in spring. The young black-back gull is speckled. Its feathers change each time it molts, and its speckles gradually disappear. Although it quickly reaches adult size, it takes four years to get its adult colors.

Walking, walking, what did I see?
A bright yellow flower peeked up at me.
"How did I get to be a weed?
Once I was just a little seed."

1

Dandelions

Each dandelion plant produces a number of flowers. Bees and insects visit the flowers for nectar and pollen, pollinating the plants as they go.

After blooming, the flowers become fluffy heads with hundreds of little seeds. Each seed has a "parachute" that floats easily in the air.

Because they are hardy, and their seeds are spread so easily, dandelions are regarded as weeds.

2

3

5

4

Walking, walking, what did I see?
A flittery butterfly fluttered at me.
"How did I come to be like this?
Once I was just a chrysalis."

1

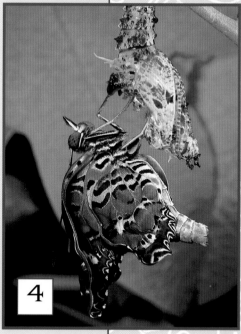

Butterflies

Butterflies lay their eggs on plants. Their eggs vary greatly in shape and size. Most eggs hatch in a few days, and the caterpillars begin eating right away.

As the caterpillar grows, it sheds its skin several times. Then the caterpillar becomes a chrysalis.

Inside the chrysalis, the butterfly forms. When it emerges, its wings are soft. Fluid is pumped through the veins, and the wings gradually grow stronger.

Walking, walking, what did I see?
An enormous crocodile grunted at me,
"Which are my babies? Can you tell?
They all look the same out of the shell!"

Crocodiles

The mother crocodile lays about forty eggs in a carefully prepared hole, and covers them over with soil. Both parents guard the eggs.

About three months later, the babies will crawl out from inside the eggs. The mother helps all the babies to hatch on the same day. She will carry the babies to the water in her mouth. Sometimes the father will help.

Crocodiles take good care of their young. They will stay with them up to three years, protecting them from predators, such as snakes, herons, raccoons, and larger crocodiles.

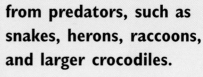

Walking, walking, what did I see?
A strange-looking creature stared at me.
"I have no wings to help me fly.
Is it true I'll become a dragonfly?"

1

Dragonflies

Dragonflies lay their eggs on water plants. The eggs hatch into nymphs that live in the pond for several years. They are fierce hunters, and eat water insects and young fish.

Eventually, the nymph becomes a pupa. Inside the pupa, the nymph gradually changes into a dragonfly. Dragonflies have large, powerful wings, and strong jaws for eating other flying insects.

Walking, walking, what did I see?
A golden oak tree whispered to me,
"My leaves, they are falling one by one.
Why are there times when I have none?"

1

2

Oak Tree

Oak trees are deciduous. This means that they lose their leaves in autumn. As the days get shorter, the leaves change color. This is because there is less of the sunlight they need to make their food. The tree is dormant. It does not grow.

When spring comes, buds appear, and soon the tree is covered with new green leaves. The cycle begins again.

3

"There's a lot
I don't know,"
I said to the tree.
"But I do know
You were here
Long before me."